Louis Weber, C.E.O.
Publications International, Ltd.
7373 North Cicero Avenue
Lincolnwood, Illinois 60646

Manufactured in U.S.A.

9 8 7 6 5 4 3 2 1

Library of Congress Catalog Card Number: 86-60772

ISBN: 1-56173-865-4

Illustrators: Nan Brooks, Laura D'Argo, Jeff Mangiat, Mike Muir

BY THE EDITORS OF CONSUMER GUIDE®

Favorite

HELPFUL HOUSEHOLD HINTS

GREAT POND PUBLISHING™

Contents

CONTENTS